MY CONVERSATION WITH

THE UNIVERSE

MY CONVERSATION WITH
THE UNIVERSE

DARRIN MASON

IB

We shall require a substantially
new manner of thinking if mankind
is to survive. – **Albert Einstein**

Beginning today, treat everyone you meet as
if they were going to be dead by midnight. Extend
to them all the care, kindness, and understanding
you can muster, and do it with no thought of any
reward. Your life will never be the same again.
– Og Mandino

CONTENTS

INTRODUCTION

IN late 2006, I watched a film called The Secret and it changed my life forever. Not because it taught me anything new, but because it reminded me of what I *already* knew, and I knew those things because they, like me, are of The Universe, the field of energy known by some as God, by others as Allah. I do not believe God or Allah to be men, nor do I believe The Universe to be anything other than what it is, a name given by the New Age movement to the field of energy that surrounds us and is us, just as God is a name given to that same field of energy by the Christians, and just as Allah is a name given to that same field of energy by the Muslims. To be fair to their beliefs, I agree with them on one big thing, that the field of energy surrounding us is the be all and end all of everything good. But none of anything is good, or bad, really. It just is. And after more than forty five years of living, the benefits of letting things be what they are instead of trying to make them into what I think they *should* be have finally dawned on me. Thank God. Or should that be, thank The Universe.

Thank you friends, and enjoy.

Darrin Mason
August, 2015

FOREWORD

My Path to Spiritual Enlightenment

I don't remember much about my late stepfather. It is, after all, more than thirty years since he passed. One thing I *do* remember, though, is he was a strict Catholic and attended Church on a regular basis. One of those times, and one of less than a handful of times I've ever been inside a Catholic Church, was while we were on a family holiday in the early 1980's (only two or three years before he passed).

We had been on the road for about a week, picked up my then-stepbrother (my late stepfather's son), and headed for the nearest Catholic Church to attend a Sunday Mass. On entering, I noticed people kneeling and crossing their chest with their hand, an obvious Catholic tradition. My brother, a Presbyterian, did the same. I, christened a Presbyterian but already on the path of spiritual wondering, did not.

It was an interesting moment in time, one that served to strengthen my resolve against having to fall in line with those whose actions I either didn't agree with or didn't believe in. I knew in my heart there was more to life than falling in line with anyone but myself so I set about finding it, or, better still, finding more of it.

That search led me through two continents, half a dozen countries, a broken marriage, two broken engagements, and several religions, one – The Church of Jesus Christ of Latter Day Saints – of which proved to be more of an eye-opener than a religion in that the atmosphere was much more relaxed than most other religions, but in all reality was not as different from most mainstream religions as it believes itself to be. An example of this being that children shall not be baptized until a certain age, but by which time they have been to the Church with their parents and aunts and uncles and older brothers and sisters so many hundreds of times it's all they know and all it takes for them to jump at the chance to be baptized a Latter Day Saint. It also took me to a Buddhist temple, and it was there that the light bulb over my head not only switched on but lit up most of the east-coast of Australia. I had at last found what I was looking for: a way of life as opposed to a religion. However, as wonderful as I found Buddhism and its message to be, it did not fully serve me. I needed more.

So I took the best that Buddhism had to offer (which was, and still is, plenty), tucked it under my arm, and set out to find it. That path took me through another broken relationship and into direct contact with a woman who introduced me, through the classes she taught and the truths she believed in, to the world of meditation. Of course I had heard of it and on the odd occasion even practiced it, but never at such close quarters to the group of people this woman was a part of.

The Benefits of Meditation

I wish to make it clear that this book is not one about meditation but a transcript of my ongoing conversation with The Universe. However, I would like it to be known too that my connection with The Universe would never have been strong enough to receive its words clearly enough to put them into a book had I not been fully enveloped by the power of meditation as it was introduced and shown to me several years ago, hence my acknowledgement of it in the first place. Funny that after all these years, after so many possible paths to follow that I ignored and went on my merry way, after so many friendships and relationships, none of which was the answer to the question of "What, why, where, who, when, and how?" that burned in my heart, it took only one person who excelled at the one thing that would truly touch me to open my eyes to everything I could possibly be.

The Light at the End of a Dark Tunnel

I can see it and feel its warmth against my skin, but to think I've reached it is to think I have nothing more to learn and nothing more to do. Nothing could be further from the truth, and if it were true they might as well take me now for the rest of my time on this planet would be too boring to live through. Instead, I have plenty to learn and plenty to do, and I have surrounded myself with likeminded people to keep me company as I learn and do them. I also have The Universe, the field of energy that has given me everything I've had so far and will give me everything I want and need in the future as I continue my life-long journey to that light at the end of a dark tunnel. To The Universe, I say thank you.

MY CONVERSATION WITH
THE UNIVERSE

What's Up with What Goes On?

Darrin: We've all wondered at one time or another why we're here. What *I* would like to know is why we have the experiences we do *while* we're here?

The Universe: Before you came to planet Earth, you signed a contract with me. In it, you agreed to every single thing that would happen to you, good or bad, as a way of learning those things you did not already know, or, better still, learning how to do them better. While many people have benefited along the way, it's true that others have been hurt in this learning and as sad as it is that this has happened, please know that they have signed their own contracts in which they also agreed to every single thing that would happen to them, good or bad, as a way of learning those things they did not already know, or, better still, learning how to do them better. That it took for both you and them to not only cross paths but also to cross swords was not a trick on my part, nor was it a joke on you or them. It is simply how it works. You see, every single thing and every single one is a part of me as I am a part of them and as it takes every single part of a Swiss watch to work in perfect harmony for the watch as a whole to work perfectly, so too does it take every single thing and every single one to work in perfect harmony for me to work perfectly, and they do, and I *know* they do because *I* do.

I know you have wondered "How perfect is it?" when you have suffered and cried and picked up the pieces of a broken heart, both yours and theirs, more times than you care to remember, but how perfect is it that you have experienced all of those things yet lived to see every new day since the day you were born, that in spite of it all you are still here, that you are deeply and truly in love with the woman you know to be the one true love of your life and your soul-mate, that you have introduced into the world two beautiful children who will come to learn their own lessons, many of them from you?

It is all connected and if you remove one thing or one person from the equation, the house of cards falls down, quite often around you, and that is the consequence you will suffer for not trusting me or in me. Please know, though, that the consequence you suffer is not me seeking vengeance on you. That is not what I'm about. It never has been and never will be. It is simply a sign that you are not in alignment with what I am and what I'm trying to give you, which is everything good. If, on the other hand, *I* remove that one thing or one person, you must let it be, because to fight it is to not trust in me and to not trust in me is to not receive those things I'm trying to give you, which again is everything good. The lesson to be learned here is to not fight for something to be what you think it should be, that is rather selfish and terribly tiresome for you, them, and for me, but let it be what it is *meant* to be. Do that and you will be pleasantly surprised at how much better things can and will be than you ever dreamed they *could* be.

Darrin: And were led by others to believe.

The Universe: You may not believe it, but the people who raised you were not bad, they simply didn't know any better. Actually, that's not quite true. They *did* know better. They simply couldn't do what they knew in their hearts to be the right thing because of their habitual ways of thinking and living, ways taught to them by an older generation who couldn't do what *they* knew in their hearts to be the right thing because of *their* habitual ways of thinking and living, ways taught to them by an even *older* generation. And guess what, you and your family are not alone. Hundreds and millions of families all over the world are as "dysfunctional" as yours was and continues to be. All of a sudden, you realize your upbringing wasn't so bad. It simply wasn't as good as it could've been, or as good as you believe it *should've* been. And therein lies the problem – you've tried to create in the reality of others, even if only by hoping things were different than they were, and no matter what, no matter how hard you try, you cannot create in another's reality, you can only make your own as attractive to them as possible (and as attractive to *yourself* as possible). And if they don't like what they see, they move on, and you let them. That some will stay and try to create in *your* reality is not and never has been lost on me, by the way. My response to that is for you to move on as it is to them in the same situation. If you don't, it's not because you don't deserve better. It's not because you're not smart enough or brave enough to do so. It's because you have a lesson to be learned from that person or that feeling or that situation, and sometimes the answer comes to you in that moment, and sometimes it comes days, months, or even years later. Sometimes it never comes at all. And that's simply how it is and how it's meant to be. And guess what? You weren't a prisoner in any of those situations. You could've left any time you wanted to. But you didn't. Again, not because you weren't smart enough or brave enough or because you didn't deserve better, but because it was written into the contract you signed with me before you came to planet Earth. And, again, when you come to realize that you are still here, that you have a job that pays the bills, and that you have two children and a woman in your life that love you truly – more truly than you have ever been loved before in this life or any other – how bad can it really have been?

How Bad *Can* It Have Been?

The Universe: It can't have for there is no such thing as good or bad. Nor is there any such thing as left or right, black or white, or up or down. There's no such thing as anything at all except what you see. Everything else is what you *perceive* it to be, based on the lessons you've learned and been taught by friends, family, and foe alike, and based on mankind's need to label everything with a word, which in itself is a form of control, rather than simply experiencing and enjoying things for what they are and what things are can only be what you know to be good because everything is *of* me. For example, does it matter if a rose is red, yellow, white or black? Can't it just be admired for what it is, and for how it smells? For how it makes you feel when you see or receive one? And now that you understand that good, bad, black, white, up, down, and every other word in every language ever spoken are just that, words, you understand too that nothing bad ever happens, as does nothing good. Everything just . . . happens. Your job is not to label those things with words, but to let them happen, and also to make the most of everything that does. To do anything else is to try and control the outcome. And we all know what happens when we do that, don't we?

Darrin: It goes from bad to worse?

The Universe: Again, they are only words. What it boils down to is how you feel. Do you feel good or do you feel bad? If you feel good, keep doing whatever it is you are doing. If you feel bad, stop doing it and don't do it again. And yes, I understand that I have used words to describe a feeling, but words are what the human race understands best so that is what I use, but that does not make those words anymore than what they are – words. That words are what the human race understands best is also why you have books, newspapers, and magazines instead of pounding drums and smoke signals like you once did (I do acknowledge that they are still in use but nowhere near as much or as often and when they are it is for entertainment purposes as much as anything else). So while I don't want you using words in a way that stops the flow of good when you are experiencing good – we can after all over analyse things which sucks the life out of the experience we are having – used correctly they are a legitimate way of delivering a message from one person to another or to many.

Now, I mentioned before that if you feel good you should keep doing whatever it is that's making you feel good. However, if what you are doing is making someone else feel bad, you should stop, or at least stop doing it in their presence, and I say that instead of telling you to stop no matter what because while what you are doing may not be bad in and of itself they may not be able to feel as good as you about whatever it is that is making you feel good. But, as I said, that doesn't mean you should stop doing it all together. If you do, you have allowed them to control you, and sooner or later you will come to resent them for it and retaliate toward them, and usually in ways you will come to regret and you will regret it because you know what you have done is detrimental to your growth as a human being . . . and theirs.

I Want to Change the World...

Darrin: I want to change the world, to leave an

impression on it. How does growing as a human being allow me to do that?

The Universe: By growing as a human being and doing things in a more appropriate (read, mature) way, you cause a ripple effect, one that affects those around you. If those around you choose to learn from your growth and therefore create their own growth, they in turn cause a ripple effect of their own which affects those around them, and so it goes and as it goes you have changed the world by doing nothing more than growing as a human being. Please let it be known too that while not everyone will want to learn and grow, you can be sure that someone somewhere does. And sooner or later you will find them.

Will I Ever Get Back More Than I Give?

The Universe: The number one rule about giving is to not want anything back because to want something back is to expect it and to expect it is to demand it, usually from the person you have given to. Let go of the expectation that when you give you will automatically get back or that you will ever get back at all because you won't always and when you do it won't always be from the person you gave to.

Enjoy the act of giving, allow that enjoyable feeling to take you over, and it will bring you into a much happier space and the happier you are the more likely others are to want to give something (back) to you. And if they don't, does it matter? Of course it doesn't, for just as giving was *your* choice, *not* giving is theirs, and to give without fear of not getting back is to prove to me that you are happy with what you had before you gave and with what you have *after* giving and that you are capable of replacing what you had and you replace it now as you gained it before and then others give also and there you are . . . getting back more than you gave.

Is There a God?

Darrin: People are forever trying to prove that God does not exist. Does the fact they are even bothering prove that God *could* exist?

The Universe: You and I both know he doesn't, that God is nothing more than a name given to the field of energy, me, that surrounds you, Darrin, and *is* you. That people would spend their time trying to prove the non-existence of something instead of enjoying those things that *do* exist, at least in their reality, is up to them and is doing no one any harm, as long as they spend it trying to prove it to themselves and not to those around them who *do* believe in the existence of those very same things. Inform them of the possibility that something might not exist, yes, but let them make up their own minds based on their own beliefs and ideals as to whether it actually does or doesn't.

Darrin: Which brings me to my next question: Destiny or free will?

The Universe: There is no such thing as destiny, not for you at least, only free will. You have a choice in whatever you do (you made it when you signed the contract before coming to planet Earth, remember?). But know that whatever you do will help create the single big picture that is *my* destiny.

Darrin: You have a destiny? What is it? And isn't us helping create the single big picture that is *your* destiny a destiny in itself?

The Universe: My destiny is to be everything I can, and I can't be that without you and every other person and every other thing that has ever graced planet Earth being everything *you* can. Just remember that while you might eventually be more than you are right now, you are being everything you can in any given moment, just as I am, and if you were meant to be more, you would be, just as I would be. I tell you that not to bring you down, but to remind you of something that will bring you down if you let it, and to be brought down in any way at any time by anyone or anything is to be less than you can be, which is to be less than you *should* be.

Darrin: You say it's up to us, but it sounds like it's really up to you. Which one is it?

The Universe: Both.

Is There a Heaven and Hell?

Darrin: One of those people who helped raise me died almost thirty years ago in a car crash. Since then, I've wondered occasionally if there's a Heaven or a Hell. Is there?

The Universe: Not in the biblical sense, just as there's no God and no Devil. So when people speak of Heaven, they are really speaking of a feeling, one so pure and true it cannot be felt on planet Earth, not even by those who are living their life to the fullest and without a single regret. It can only be achieved by your body passing into death and your spirit becoming one with me once again, free of the negativity and pain and sorrow you are sure to feel and can only feel there on planet Earth. That you are sure to feel it and can only feel it on planet Earth means then that Hell must therefore be, and is, life on planet Earth where you are surrounded by that negativity and pain and sorrow. It is fair then to say that the one you speak of who helped raise you and died almost thirty years ago became free of that negativity and pain and sorrow upon the death of his physical body and was therefore able to reconnect with me, and he has. He is once more pure energy; just as every person who ever lived once again becomes pure energy when *their* bodies pass into death.

Now that you know there is no Heaven or Hell (in the biblical sense at least), and that those whose bodies have passed into death have become one with me once more, you may rest easy that the one you speak of was what he was to you only there on planet Earth and, as I alluded to earlier, what happens on planet Earth is neither good or bad, black or white, up or down, round or flat. Everything is only what you perceive it to be, and the fact you perceived him to be bad is a reflection of the fact you recognized in your heart from an early age what you believed to be good, and you strove for it, and you reached it, and you achieved it. Not everyone is so fortunate, and those that aren't are those that are sent back time and again until they get it right. That said, please don't think you got it right first time, and don't think you won't ever be sent back again even after getting it right, because even those who eventually get it right are returned to planet Earth many times after that to act as a foil if you will to those who've yet to get it right. After all, if there were only what the human race has labelled bad people capable of bad things inhabiting planet Earth, they would eventually wipe themselves out, leaving nothing and no one for them to come back to so they might learn the lessons they are yet to learn.

Darrin: Having read that, a cynic might suggest you are wanting to create more of the good for no other reason than you might gorge on it, that it's the only way for you to become more than what you are. Would they be right?

The Universe: The universe as thought of and seen by astronomers, scientists, and the like is expanding at a phenomenal rate. It is feeding on something. That something is the good the human spirit returns to it with, just as I am expanding in the hearts and minds of the human race at a phenomenal rate with the same thing. That is no bad thing on my part as your cynic might think or suggest, but progress toward a total utopia where there is no need for the human spirit to return to planet Earth for further learning and growth because it will already have achieved all that is possible and it will have done so by feeding off me as I have off it. In other words, and to put it more simply, you scratch my back, I'll scratch yours. We both benefit, and we both win.

Darrin: But you seem to benefit more. I mean, you are expanding and the human race will eventually become extinct.

The Universe: But the human race is *of* me. Indeed, it is as much a part of me as the planets and stars and galaxies and everything else seen by the human eye and everything that will never be seen by *any* eye. How then can it ever become anything but more of the good *I* become? Just because we feed off each other, and we do, doesn't mean I'm going to devour it. It simply means the good that I am, that the human spirit becomes one with when a person's body passes into death, will, as I said, help it become so great there will be one day no need for it to return to planet Earth for all its lessons will have been learned. That's the day the human race will become extinct.

Darrin: Would you like to give us a time frame?

The Universe: No, and I'll tell you why: There is no such thing as time. It is nothing but a word thought up by a member of the human race to describe the line that connects one dot to another, one event to another. And because time doesn't exist, how can one possibly put a time frame on anything? Is it any wonder then that those who succeed most are those who let go of the expectation that something will happen, and should happen, by a certain "time" and simply let things happen when they are meant to, that they trust the natural order of things as determined by me? Know I have never done wrong by any of you, and never will, for you are me and I am you so trust the natural order of things as those who succeed most have and continue to do and you will succeed also. And now that you know, feel free to get rid of the watch once and for all and let your feelings and emotions point you to where you're going instead. Let *that* happen and you begin to enjoy the world around you instead of needing to control it. Enjoy the world around you and it won't only be your oyster, it will be the pillow of air on which you shall float from where you are to where you are meant to be.

Darrin: And where am I meant to be?

The Universe: Wherever you want. If you want to be a doctor, *be* a doctor. If you want to be a police officer, *be* a police officer. If you want to sit around and do nothing all day, then do it. But know there are consequences for everything you do. If you become a doctor, the consequence is that you might occasionally get blood on your hands. If you become a police officer, the consequence is that you might occasionally have to shoot someone, or that you might be shot. If you choose to sit around and do nothing all day, the consequence is that you will probably end up overweight and with nothing in the bank. If that's what you want, go for it. But if you don't want to end up overweight and with nothing in the bank then you had better not sit around all day doing nothing. If you don't want to get blood on your hands or have to shoot someone, or be shot by them, then don't become a doctor or a police officer. But if the desire to save lives, or protect them, is greater than not wanting to get blood on your hands or having to shoot someone, or be shot by them, by all means become a doctor or a police officer. And that's what it boils down to, that you don't have to love what you do; you just have to find a better reason for doing it than *not* doing it. And that doesn't just apply to work either. It applies to relationships, friendships, food, pets, everything.

There will be those of course who think that by doing something for no reason other than you found a better reason to do it than to *not* do it you are being selfish, that you are holding someone else who truly loves it back from doing it, but you aren't. You only become selfish when you are doing something with the sole purpose of holding someone else back, in which case you are also being silly, because the time and energy spent on doing something so someone else can't have it is not being spent doing something that will make you and your life better than it was before you started doing it.

What about Past Lives?

Darrin: It's said we don't remember our past lives when we come back for the next one. First of all, do we remember them, and second of all, after everything bad that may have happened in a previous life, why would we want to remember it anyway?

20

The Universe: You all live multiple lives, mostly because you haven't yet learned all the lessons in past lives you set yourself to learn in the contract you signed, but also because you play your own part in helping *others* learn the lessons they set *themselves* to learn, lessons they *too* are yet to have learned. And as far as remembering past lives is concerned, consciously you don't, but subconsciously you remember everything, you know everything, and you feel everything. To remember everything, to know everything, and to feel everything on a conscious level would be to confuse a race who was not made to know or feel anything but that which is happening in the now. That they try to know or feel anything but that which is happening in the now is folly on their part and leads only to confusion and chaos in their minds and that which is in their minds is made to become real in their eyes and in their hands. Best then to focus on all things good and you know something is good because it makes you feel good. And just because it doesn't make you feel good all the time doesn't mean it's bad, either. It really just is what it is, and you not feeling good in spite of having it might simply be a reflection of the fact there is something in you that is not functioning as it should, and you fix it first by owning what is causing the problem, for you are the only one that can remove what is causing it and you do that by owning it.

Once what has caused the problem has been owned, you repair the damage and you do that first with your mind. You go to a psychologist to fix a psychological problem, you go to a doctor to fix a physical ailment, and you do these things just as you would call someone in to replace a broken window, or just as you would call a mechanic to fix a car whose engine won't start. After all, you don't leave the window broken and you don't leave the car to not start, just as you don't leave a psychological ailment, or a physical one, unattended. But you don't blame others for those problems either. You might point the finger at whoever broke the window, and you might eventually be compensated for the damage they caused, but your first priority is to replace the window, at least it should be, just as your first priority should be to have the ailment, be it psychological or physical, attended to as soon as possible. And if the ailment has been caused directly by someone else (e.g. physical or emotional abuse), let the police deal with the legal side of it, let the doctor deal with the physical or psychological side of it, and let *me* deal with the spiritual side of it. Your only job is to draw our attention to it, and you can only do that by acknowledging there is a problem, and you do that by owning it. That doesn't mean others won't pay the price if they have played a part in the creation of the problem. One way or another, they will. Just don't let yourself be concerned, or worse, consumed, by it. To be either of those things will only cause you to be stressed, and stress on any part of you, as it does if you put enough stress on a stick or a car or a house or a ship, will break you.

Why Are There So Many Religions?

Darrin: If there is only one God, as most religions claim there to be, why are there so many religions?

The Universe: Because there are so many different types of man. Just as there are a thousand different novels by a thousand different authors for a thousand different groups of people to read, there are a thousand different religions created by a thousand different men for a thousand different groups of people to believe in. The thing about all of that is they all espouse one common message, that there is a supreme being called God who had a son called Jesus who died on the cross and was resurrected three days later. The thing about all of that is they all espouse another common message, that their religion is the only true religion. Its like a ratings war between two or more television news programs that are on different channels at the same time reporting the same story from sometimes the same angle but at other times different angles and who think that the more people who watch them the better and truer they must be than the other news program(s). Life, love, and religion are not popularity contests, people, and I wish everyone would get that.

Would My Life Be Better or Worse?

Darrin: Would my life be better or worse if I knew the day, time, and place I was going to die?

The Universe: It would be what it is. If I told you now that you were going to die in an airplane crash over the mountains of Colorado at 7 p.m. on March 5, 2018, would you stop flying between now and then? No. If anything, you would want to live an even fuller life than the one you are living now. In fact, you would probably even fly more often between now and then. You would take greater risks than you otherwise would. And all because you knew you weren't going to die until March 5, 2018. But others will not take that risk, they will not fly more often, they will not tempt fate, all out of fear that to tempt fate would be to increase the chance of dying *before* March 5, 2018. In that case, life would be worse because they are now living less of a life than they otherwise would out of fear that to live more of a life would be to tempt fate. I do not apologize for saying that is a horrible space to be in because it is.

The point is that your life would be better or worse depending on how you see things, on whether or not you see the good or bad in them, on whether you are an optimist or a pessimist. See the good in everything around you and reach for it. You may not always get it, but I can and will guarantee that you will always, and I mean always, end up with more than you began with. Also remember this life will come to an end eventually (I can and will guarantee that too), and while your body may not die a pleasant death, it is much better to die having lived a pleasant life. Trust me.

As A Race, How Old Are We?

Darrin: Were we born thousands of years ago of Adam and Eve as some Churches would have us believe? Are we born of life on other planets as the Church of Scientology would have us believe? Or are we a cake of one flavour or another that has been mixed by you and is being cooked over a period of time?

The Universe: You are as old as me for you are *of* me, not of the loins of Adam and the vagina of Eve or anyone else, be they of planet Earth or any other planet in your galaxy or any other galaxy for that matter. And if you really wish to know when man first walked planet Earth, it was September 3, 45,202 BC at 3.17pm and twenty-five seconds.

Darrin: You're kidding, right?

The Universe: Yes I am. The point I am making is it doesn't matter. So much time is wasted by so many trying to prove so little they miss the opportunity to prove the only thing that truly matters is now.

Darrin: I get that, and I agree with it, but for the sake of my growth and that of this book, I have more questions to ask of you. First of all, how old am I, Darrin Mason?

The Universe: Again, you are as old as me for you are *of* me. You might in fact be wondering how old your *body* is, that which came to be so many months or years ago and that which will surely one day die. Please don't confuse you and your body for they are as different as chalk and cheese. And as old as your body is, never forget there were others here before you. As old as your body is, never forget there are others who are wiser than you. And as old as your body is, never forget there will always be someone better than you at those things you thought you were the best at. By doing those things, and more things like it, you are showing your ability to be humble, and the more humble one is the less humble one needs to be.

Darrin: And how old would my *body* be if it didn't know how old it was?

The Universe: It would be what it is, and what it clearly is not is a number. On the other hand, what it clearly is, besides what you see in the mirror each time you look into it, is a house for your spirit while it is having its human experience. That's what it is, and as special as that is, it's *all* it is. And the sooner you come to realize the number of years you have been here in this life is irrelevant to anything but society's expectation that you behave the same way as others your 'age' behave, the sooner you realize you do not have to behave in any way other than that which will bring you the most good while doing the least harm to those around you. There are those who won't believe that. Please don't be one of them.

Make Love Not War...

Darrin: Why do religions that support love cause so many wars?

The Universe: Religions don't cause wars. The people who are in charge of them do. The problem is they don't see it, and therefore make no attempt to stop it, because they weren't the ones who started it. What they don't understand is they have pushed their self-serving beliefs so hard on others that those other people have been brainwashed into starting the war on their behalf.

Can We Be and Have Anything We Want?

Darrin: What if I want to be rich? Will I be?

The Universe: Of course. But if all you ask for is to be rich, you must accept that rich does not only apply to financial wealth and because it doesn't you might find yourself rich in other areas of your life than the one you were thinking which more often than not is financially. Instead, it might be in your love life, in your job, or in any one of your friendships. And to be rich in any of those is to be as rich as you would be if you were rich financially.

The problem most people have with that will be that they wanted money in the bank and think it will turn up just by wanting to be rich but have not been specific about the area of their life they want to be rich in and then get upset when someone else makes the money which only further distances them from the financial wealth they were wanting and also from the richness in their love life, their job, or in any one of their friendships I have delivered to them.

It's better to want success, for success is that which riches naturally follow. To want it any other way is to want riches handed to you on a platter, and nothing handed to anyone on a platter was ever truly appreciated, no matter what anyone who ever received anything on a platter would have you believe.

Friends Come and Go...

Darrin: Friends come and go. So do relationships for that matter. Why don't they just stay?

The Universe: There is only so much we can learn from one person, or need to. We experience growth from our learning and so do they, and not always in the same direction. Therefore, and sometimes even when the growth is in the same direction, the people that come will inevitably go, even if only for a period of time (couples separate and come back together again, friends part ways only to bump into each other years later), and sometimes for all time. As unfortunate or unfair as it might seem, it isn't really. It is all a part of my bigger picture of which each and every one of you has a part to play. The only unfortunate thing, if there ever is one, is that some don't play their part as well as others play their's. They are the ones who return to planet Earth time and again until their lessons have been learned.

Darrin: Why is it that couples can separate then come back together? Why is it that neither of them moves on to someone else in the meantime?

The Universe: Sometimes they do, sometimes they don't. Sometimes they want to but never find the person they're looking for so return to their former partner in life and love. That is not always a good idea. That said, it isn't always a bad one either. Also, and this is most important, their time apart is an opportunity to regroup, to gather their thoughts and emotions, to grow stronger in love by realizing how much in love with the other person they truly are. Their time apart can also be spent feeling sorry for themselves, and as a result they are unable to best utilize the time I have afforded them to gather their thoughts and emotions so they might be stronger in love when I bring them back together. And sometimes I bring them back together when things are not good for either of them to remind them of why I pulled them apart in the first place, that it is indeed time to move onto other people, permanently.

But remember this – things not being good for either or both at any time whether they are together or apart doesn't mean they aren't meant to be together or apart. It simply means they are in that moment experiencing a lesson to learn that will ultimately see them be where they are meant to be, and not you or anyone else knows where they are meant to be except for in the moment so just accept where you are for if you weren't meant to be where you are you wouldn't be there.

So next time you wish you were somewhere else, and maybe even with some-*one* else, remember that you are where you are, and with who you're with, for a reason, because I determined you needed to be where you are, and with who you're with, for every other thing to happen so every other thing after that can happen also, and maybe, just maybe, if you stayed there I wouldn't have to keep putting you back where you were, or with who you've been with, time after time, because you'd already be there.

Darrin: And what if the reason they keep parting is because they don't understand or won't believe their time has come and they keep coming back together for no other reason than *they* think they should be together?

The Universe: What you think and what you feel are two different things. What you feel creates your thoughts. What you think, on the other hand, creates your actions. Beware, for your choice to return to someone you have separated from time after time is not always fuelled by good feelings or good thoughts. They are sometimes created by negative feelings of envy or pride or downright selfishness, and those feelings create negative thoughts of envy or pride or downright selfishness. That negative thought is usually not seen as negative though because the person thinking it is thinking habitually. They have been taught by those who came before them to think and feel that way and that the way they are thinking and feeling is normal, and they will always think and feel that way unless and until they are able to see the thought for what it truly is, negative, and unless and until they can that negative thought will hold them back forever. When they have seen it for what it truly is, though, and they will only be able to do so by removing themselves physically, emotionally, spiritually and mentally from those who came before them, they are then able to release that thought into the nether regions of space where it will be engulfed by the goodness from which it first came and they will accept that it only became negative once it entered the mind of someone who was taught by those who came before them that nothing was their fault and everything was someone else's fault, but they now know that while everything might not be their fault, they are responsible for their own actions. The void where there was once a negative thought can then be filled with a positive one, but only if they have removed themselves physically, emotionally, spiritually and mentally from those who came before them for those who came before them would seek to control them and their way of life and to fill that void with more negative thoughts, and know the need to control is a vicious desire that will do no one any good, ever. Recognize that and you recognize the need to leave them behind forever.

And for those who think they know everything and can do it all themselves, here's the kick in the pants: among those you need to leave behind, among those who would stand tallest in the way of who you want to be, is you, and not the you of the future (the one who has left behind those who would do you wrong because that's all they knew), but the one of the past who has done you wrong because that's all *he* knew.

Darrin: If only I knew then what I know now . . .

The Universe: But you've *always* known (subconsciously, at least) everything there is to know, then and now, and you've known it consciously when you've *needed* to know. And that's most people's problem: they've wanted to know something when they thought *they* should know, instead of letting *me* let them know when they actually *needed* to know. If you're still not sure, think of it like a tap. The water is always there, but it only comes out when you turn the tap on, and you only turn the tap on when you need the water. But guess what? I'm the one who turns the tap on and off and I do it when the time is right, not when you *think* its right.

So, again, let go of the need to control and just enjoy the moment. And above all, trust that what is happening in each moment is what is *meant* to happen. After all, if it wasn't meant to be happening, it wouldn't be. Remember?

Darrin: Two people close to me have cancer. Was that meant to happen?

The Universe: Again, if it wasn't meant to happen, it wouldn't. So the answer to your question is, yes. But I'm thinking that what you are *really* wondering is *why* it's happening, like, "Why do bad things happen to good people?" That is a fair question. But then again, who says cancer is bad? Yes, it can result in death, but death, while sad, is not always bad and to not want someone to die, to want them here for your purpose instead of mine is to be selfish, for the part they have to play in my bigger picture is greater than it will ever be in yours. Of course, people with cancer don't always die either. You must remember that. Indeed, many of them survive this life changing experience and go on to bigger and better things, different things, for their life to that moment has served its purpose, and mine, and a new direction is needed. That new direction can be taken by way of a relationship breakdown, the loss of a job, or getting, and surviving, cancer. The person having that experience becomes then a much stronger person in their fight for survival, a strength that will serve them well somewhere down the track. The new direction can also be taken by way of *not* surviving a car accident or by *not* beating a deadly disease. It may be that the body their soul inhabited has been abused emotionally or physically beyond any reasonable repair. It may be that the people around them are better served by that person not being there. And it may be that someone else, perhaps in another part of the world or another moment in time, will be better served by having that person in *their* life, and the only way for that to happen is for that person to pass over and to be reborn into another body in another part of the world or another moment in time. Whatever the reason, to quote Dr Seuss, it's better to be happy they were there at all than to cry because it's over, and to want them back from the dead is to want them back so you don't feel so sad, and to do that is to be selfish, and selfishness is a thought that creates a feeling that creates an action that does no one any good. Not now, not ever.

Darrin: All of that sounds like them getting cancer was your choice, not theirs, yet you said earlier that we agreed to everything that would ever happen to us. Surely they wouldn't have agreed to get cancer, would they?

The Universe: Each of your lives on planet Earth are but single strokes of the brush on the bigger picture that is me. Remember the saying, "You are not a human being having a spiritual experience, but a spirit having a human experience". If part of that human experience – which is nothing more than a series of lessons learned (or *not* learned as the case may be) – is getting cancer, so be it. Be strong enough, and trusting enough of me, to know that I know cancer can kill and it often does, but that your suffering through it, either as the person who has it or is close to someone who does, is the lesson to be learned, the experience to be had, or the pain and loss to be suffered, by those that learn it, experience it, or suffer it, because they are the ones best able to cope with it, to get over it, and get on with life.

Darrin: There are those who *didn't* cope with it, *or* get over it, *or* get on with it that would disagree with you.

The Universe: That they are alive to tell the tale means they *did* cope with it, they *did* get over it, and they *did* get on with it. That they think they didn't is a reflection of their inability to break free of the habitual negative way of thinking they have inherited from those who came before them. Yet all they have to do is recognize the fact they are alive to understand how good things are for them. That they don't get that, that they don't see it, is unfortunate but not getting it and not seeing it are what you might call necessary evils that help create me and help create everything that happens.

Just be happy you *do* get it, that you *do* see it, that you *do* understand how good things are for you. Let those who don't get it or see it lay in that bed all alone. You have bigger fish to fry.

Darrin: Such as?

The Universe: You don't yet know? Of course you do. It was in your contract. Remember? Your bigger fish to fry is that which is in your heart, that which you feel with every beat of it. You breathe it, day in, day out. You long for it from the moment you wake until the moment you go to sleep. Then, while you are asleep, you dream of it. And it's something different for everyone. For some it's raising a family. For others it's creating a successful business. For others still, it's enforcing the law or saving lives. The problem is that so many people don't realize that's what it is and that's *all* it is. They "slave away", feeling for sure there must be more to life, and not getting that the something more they feel for sure will turn up as long as they keep slaving away will come if only they enjoyed what they were doing in the now, that happy thoughts create happy feelings which create a happy life. And that's it. That's what you want. That's what *all* of you want and it's *all* you want: *a happy life.* And you have it by enjoying what you are doing in any given moment, whether it's raising a family, or creating a business, or enforcing the law or saving lives. It's as simple as that.

What's the Deal with Celebrity?

Darrin: I get that everyone plays their part in the bigger picture, but why is it that some play a more *public* part than others?

The Universe: Not everyone is in tune with what I have to say, so I sometimes say it through songs, books, movies, and so on. And if you don't believe me, think about it for a moment. How often have the words of a song or a line from a movie resonated with you, and others, and made you go, "So *that's* what it means"? Or you've looked at those singers and songwriters and authors and scriptwriters and thought, "Where do they come up with that?" It comes from me, just as the words in this book have. You, as it is with those who write the songs, books, and movie scripts that stop people in their tracks and make them think, are in tune with me, and know how fortunate you are to be so, not because your ability to write a book or tell a story or communicate a thought has the potential to earn you a lot of money, but because your ability to write a book or tell a story or communicate a thought is my gift to you as it is to the world *through* you, just as a doctor's ability to save a life or a sportsman's ability to entertain on the field is my gift to them as it is to the world through *them*. There are those who look at those around them and think they don't have it as good as them, that those around them are better off because they live in mansions and drive new cars paid for by the sale of hundreds of thousands of books or albums of songs or bottoms on cinema seats. They are the ones who are not in tune with me, and they are the ones the songs are written for, the ones the books are written for, and the ones the movies are made for, and a few dollars for a book or an album or a cinema ticket isn't a whole heap of money to pay for something as valuable (or invaluable as the case may be) as anywhere from several hundred to several tens of thousands of inspiring and informative words laid out in an informative, entertaining and easy-to-understand way. Is it?

40

As for the sportsmen, and women, and the doctors and nurses and police officers who entertain people and save lives and enforce the laws, it is true that what they know has been learned in person from those around them, but it has also been learned from reading textbooks or watching film of sportspeople from another time. Ultimately, while learning from those who came before them, they have learned through those who create and it is the creators of the world who write the books and the songs and make the movies that carry my message that many of you take for granted. That does not make those who create the be all and end all of everything, for even *they* had to learn from someone, and it's not just through books and songs and movies that my message is carried. What it *does*, though, is make them a very important part of what makes the world go round. Indeed, more important than a lot of people give them credit for. But as important as they are so too are the police officers and doctors and nurses and even street cleaners for without them we would have anarchy and chaos and death and streets littered with rubbish. And pity those who think any one person or occupation is more important than another because to think that is to put one's self on a pedestal from which one might fall and might also hurt themselves when they hit the ground, and you might get just as hurt when you put yourself *beneath* another, for you look at that other with a level of disdain, a level of envy and even hatred and you rattle their tree in the hope they might fall from it and occasionally they do and when they do they usually fall on top of the person who shook the tree, hurting them in the process, and then the person who shook the tree blames the person who fell out of it for falling on top of them. Holy moly and Heaven help them.

You are all equal and you all play an equal part in creating the bigger picture. Those who still don't believe that were simply taught not to by those who came before them and have developed the negative, habitual way of thinking that will see them now and forever fall short of everything they can be and it will see them continue to take for granted the books and songs and movies I have had others make for them, those same books and songs and movies that carry my message to the world. And it's a message that, sadly, and because of their ignorance, might never reach much of its intended target.

Darrin: But if what they are being in any given moment is what they are *meant* to be in any given moment, how can they be falling short of everything they can be?

The Universe: Just because they are what they are in any given moment, doesn't mean they can't be more. If it did they have either underestimated their potential or overestimated it. Either way, shame on them.

What Price Money, Power and Control?

Darrin: There are those who will kill for power and money and control. Why?

The Universe: Because they think power and money and control is what being everything you can be is all about, and yes they might have had it all for a while – a few years, maybe even a few decades – but sooner or later each and every one of them, think Hitler and Hussein and Gaddafi and bin Laden, has been caught up with by those whose job it is to maintain the balance between what the human race has labelled right and wrong then killed. They lived life as *they* believed it should be lived, not as *I* believe it should be lived, and paid the ultimate price for it.

Darrin: You punish those who are evil by having them killed?

The Universe: No. Mankind does. That it has seen fit to give itself permission to punish those they consider evil by killing them was never my choice, nor would it ever be.

Darrin: You can't stop them?

The Universe: To do so would be to control them, and to control them would make me no better than anyone else who tries to control another.

Darrin: So you just let things . . . happen?

The Universe: Things happen as they are meant to, in the exact order they are meant to, at the exact moment they are meant to.

Darrin: To what end other than a total utopia, and what good is a utopia anyway if men are killing each other to achieve it?

The Universe: If I told you, and you told those around you, which is to be expected because news is meant to be shared (that's why you have newspapers and radios and television), and you or those around you didn't think it benefited you or suited you or your ambitions, or of those around you, I've no doubt you or any of them would likely want to change things, not that you could, to better suit you, or them, but you shouldn't do that even if you could because you would be guilty of trying to control me and trying to control me makes you no better than those who have tried to control you. You will have long ago returned to me, as will those around you, by the time the end comes anyway, so why worry about what might or might not happen in the long run, or even in the past for that matter? Better to enjoy the now.

Darrin: But the now isn't always enjoyable. Is it?

The Universe: Compared to what, the past? After all, the past is the only thing you can compare the now to, isn't it? I mean, what else *could* you compare it to, the life of the person standing or sitting next to you? Perhaps. But know there's always someone worse off than you, no matter where you're at, and even then they may not be worse off because while they may not have as much food on their plate or water in their glass, they are thinking better or happier thoughts than you, and better and happier thoughts will always create a better and happier life. After all, happiness is not about how much you have on the outside, it's about how much you have on the inside, and whilst ever you have enough on the inside the now can never be anything *but* enjoyable.

Darrin: If only we all understood that, there'd be no wars, no fights, no arguments, no nothing.

The Universe: People will *always* find something to fight about. It's human nature, unfortunately. But it balances out the good, and without something to balance them the scales tip one way or the other until they fall over. And when they *do* fall over . . . well, let's just say, better not to be under them.

Darrin: Why can't we just balance something good with something better? Why does it have to be with something bad?

The Universe: Who said that something bad isn't being balanced by something good, and that something good *isn't* being balanced by something better? People look at what they perceive to be good and see it followed by something they perceive to be bad. Why not look at something bad and see it followed by something good? Indeed, why not look at something bad and *see* something good? After all, there's something good in everything, right? Of course there is, and I *know* there is because I created it. It's only made to look bad by what you see in your head instead of what you feel in your heart and what you see in your head is determined by what you've seen on planet Earth whereas what you feel in your heart has been put there by me.

Optimism and Pessimism...

Darrin: But surely some things *are* bad, such as a shark taking a swimmer, or a dog biting the face of a child?

The Universe: Or someone close to you getting cancer? They are all bad experiences, sure, but the shark and the dog aren't doing anything other than what their instincts are *telling* them to do, and somewhere in all of that, the optimist, that wonderful person who simply cannot be distracted from the good in everything he sees, can see the good in everything, even in a shark taking a swimmer or a dog biting the face of a child. I know you are wondering how there can possibly be any good in the two examples you just gave. There isn't, at least not as you know good to be. What there is though is a simple fact: the better you feel about life in general the better you will feel in moments when sharks take swimmers and dogs bite the faces of children and the better you feel the sooner you will feel even better in spite of what has happened and the sooner you feel better the sooner you see the good around you and the sooner you realize that what happened was story and what you see around you now in spite of story, a great white shark or a dog, are beautiful creatures that did nothing more than what their instincts told them to do. That is the optimist, the one who can see something good not so much in everything that happens, but in everything in spite of what happens around them. The pessimist, on the other hand, sees the great white shark or the dog as killers because others of their kind have killed. Never mind the great white shark might be contained in an aquarium where it can do no harm or the dog is wearing a muzzle so it cannot bite. And never mind that the pessimist will only ever become more ignorant of the beauty around him because like will always attract like and when you are ignorant of anything let alone something you can only ever be more ignorant of it. That is the pessimist, the one who can see only bad not only in that which happens around him, but in everything that happens even before it does.

The good news is though you are all optimists at one time or another. The better news is some of you are optimists for all time and it is you, the eternal optimist, whose job it is to lead the way for those who aren't.

Is There Life On Other Planets?

Darrin: Is there life on other planets, or is it just us here on Earth? And you said earlier that we have all lived past lives. Do we also live *parallel* lives? If so, are the two, past and parallel, related?

The Universe: To believe you are the only form of life in an energy field stretching far beyond that which even the most powerful telescope man will ever build can see is to assume an importance in the bigger picture that you are neither entitled to or even deserve. That said, there is not another life form that takes the exact human form that those on planet Earth do, but do not for one moment believe, or even think, that it makes you any more or less special than any other life form on any other planet. It is important to note too that you have never seen those other life forms or ever will. Yes you have seen objects in the sky – craft that are thousands of years more technologically advanced than anything in the now – that can not immediately and to the untrained eye be explained, but none of them have ever contained life from another planet. What they *have* contained is a human being from another *time* (yes, those little green men with big black eyes are as human as you or any of the other billions of people who have walked the face of planet Earth). You see, extra-terrestrials have never travelled in flying discs and do not have green bodies and big black eyes. But humans of the *future* – as humans of the now have evolved from apes – have evolved from humans of the now to become the little green men with big black eyes people have seen in the flying discs the little green men with big black eyes have built using the technology of the future they travelled back from. And if you believe it's impossible to build such machines – and it is using today's technology – think about how fast technology is moving and *has* moved over a period of only a hundred years. For example, a hundred years ago, the Wright brothers pedalled a plane through the air only a few feet above the ground. Sixty years later, you sent a machine to the moon and landed it safely. The men who walked its surface were then returned safely to planet Earth. Forty years after that there are man-made machines flying around the Earth taking photos of galaxies hundreds of millions of miles away. If all this can be achieved in the space of a century, imagine what can be achieved in the space of one or two hundred of them. And if you can't, if you can't believe that man can achieve something so grand over a relatively short period of time, it's best to leave the development of the world to those who can. Regarding the second part of your question, do people live parallel lives as well as past ones, yes they do, but only in their imagination, but even then they are not imagining a parallel life as such, only a future one, or one that might have been in that moment had they made a different choice in the past to the one they made.

The truth is there is only one now and there is only one reality. Everything else is either in one's memory or their imagination.

The Power of Imagining...

Darrin: We can imagine the future we want, but can we really create it, as said by some people? As said by you?

The Universe: Albert Einstein, one of planet Earth's greatest ever minds, once said that imagination is the preview of life's coming attractions, and it is, for without something having been imagined it cannot be created and if it is not created it cannot exist. I believe what you are *really* wanting to ask is do you create the event by imagining it, or are you previewing an event that will happen regardless of whether you imagine it or not? The answer is, both. First of all, you *do* create an event by imagining it, for without the original thought, you cannot take the next necessary steps to create the event in your reality or anyone else's. Second of all, it *is* possible to preview an event that will happen regardless of whether you are the one who eventually creates it or not. For example, two people can have the same thought, one after the other for the first person has dismissed it for whatever reason or has soon forgotten it, and as thoughts are like things – that every single thought as every single thing belongs to someone, somewhere – that thought will surely and soon enough pass onto the next person who is perhaps in a better position to make good use of it and therefore make it happen, and will.

Who Decides What Is Real?

The Universe: Are you seeing a red car, or are you seeing what someone has *told* you is a red car? Just because someone says it's so, doesn't make it so. And just because more than one someone said it's so, doesn't make it anymore so than if only one person had said it.

As long as you aren't hurting anyone by believing something or *in* something you are entitled to believe anything or in anything you want. And don't let them fool you into thinking you are hurting them just because you've chosen not to believe them or in what they believe in. That is highly selfish on their part and incredibly ignorant of them to boot for there is a difference between being hurt intentionally by someone else and feeling hurt by another's actions because of your own insecurities and the difference is big, and until they realize the difference you are better staying away from them in the first place and at all times.

Darrin: Then why do so many people believe it must be real just because the majority says it is?

The Universe: Because they are brainwashed soldiers recruited to a clone army created by the demons of the past who's only hope to live on is to live through those they have brainwashed into thinking something must be real just because the majority says it is.

Darrin: Lemmings, each of them following the one in front.

The Universe: And none of them knows where the others are going. Fortunate then are those who have no need to follow another. Even more fortunate are those who not only have no need to follow another but who know where they are going.

Darrin: And even more fortunate again are those who know how to get there...

The Universe: Yes. And if you don't know, ask someone who does, and trust that they do. But before you can get to where you want to go, you must know where you are at all times even if where you are isn't nice. Many people don't know where they are because they know that to open their eyes to where they are is to open them to something they will not like. Better then to keep them shut and wander aimlessly.

Darrin: Until you run into something, that is. *Then* you'll open your eyes.

The Universe: Not always, because that something might be the front end of a moving vehicle or the jaws of a great white shark and both of them can and will kill you. Out of sight might mean out of mind, but out of sight does not always mean out of danger.

Darrin: I feel for those without the courage to face the bad things in life so they might better appreciate the good (and therefore be able to experience it).

The Universe: Don't worry, they have the courage. Underneath all those layers of the onion you yourself have managed to peel away is everything for everyone. That they won't face the bad things in life is not a reflection of a lack of courage but a reflection of their inability to believe they are better than the bullies would have them believe they are. And while you feel for them don't ever feel sorry for them.

Darrin: You can only do so much for them, right?

The Universe: Right, and don't ever lose sight of the things you need to do for yourself while you're doing what you can for them. Some people are born to live a needless life so others might live a better one, Mother Teresa is a classic example, but that's not so for everyone. It's okay to give to you and its okay to *not* give to others. Just don't keep it all to yourself out of fear you won't have enough or because you think others *already* have enough (that is both selfish and judgemental). And it *is* okay to never give so much that you have nothing left for you. Please remember that, for to give to others to the point of having nothing left for you is to leave the world no better off than it was before. Either way, you have one with nothing and one with something. Better that both have something even if both don't have the same.

What of Psychics and Premonitions?

Darrin: Some psychics I know have been remarkably close to the mark in their assessment of both my past and my future. Others, however, have landed their arrows somewhere on the other side of town from where the target is. I've also met people who have 'predicted' the future to one extent or another, me included.

Are psychics real and, in regard to your earlier comment, that a thought will surely and soon enough pass onto the next person who is perhaps in a better position to make good use of it and therefore make it happen, are they, or those who have premonitions, duty-bound to refer what will happen to the police who might then be able to stop it from happening?

The Universe: I've said it before and I'll say it again, that if it wasn't meant to happen it wouldn't.

56

Aside from the fact the police, or any other person or group of people in any position of power or authority for that matter, tend to scoff at those who have visions of the future, and they do, those who see future events have no proof that those events will happen at a particular place or a particular time or that they will happen to the people they have seen. While it is likely they will happen to those people, it is also possible, as I *also* said earlier, the vision may be someone else's and while you are seeing a dark-haired woman laying dead on a sheet of glass, she may not be anyone *you* know but someone that someone *else* knows who let that thought go and it came into your mind from there and that's why you, and others, occasionally have the feeling when you see something in your mind not of impending danger or death for you or someone you know but that you know somewhere out there someone with dark hair is or will one day be laying dead on a sheet of glass.

You should also know the best thing to do about those things you see in your vision is nothing for there is nothing you *can* do. There is also nothing the *police* can do because it hasn't happened yet and you have no names or addresses to give them or even a time so what *can* they do? It's best then to let it go and get on with your life. Of course, if and when your vision comes knocking on your door and hits you in the face you have no choice *but* to confront it and you must then deal with it as best you can. If it knocks on someone else's door, you help *them* as best you can. Just remember though, if you don't hear the knock it doesn't mean there hasn't been one, it just means the door the vision knocked on wasn't yours or someone close to you. For that you must be grateful.

The Law of Attraction...

Darrin: You have already mentioned the Law of Attraction. Over the last few years it has hit the commercial big time in a very big way thank s to the likes of Rhonda Byrne who created The Secret. What are your thoughts on the commercialization of such an important universal law?

The Universe: That is has been brought to the attention of the world is no bad thing regardless of who did it and how. The problem though for those who believe in the "ask, believe, receive" rhetoric espoused by certain people (Rhonda Byrne being one of them, and while her book The Secret was a master stroke of marketing and publicity, it should not be confused with the Law of Attraction for one is a product and the other a universal law) is they believe that as long as you ask for it and believe you will have it you must and will therefore receive it and that is an under-estimation of the bigger picture painted by me. They have created their *own* big picture, one that is framed by greed and selfishness, one that will never allow them to live life to its fullest because they are focused only on receiving that which they have asked for and want to receive.

You see, sometimes you have to receive those things you *don't* want, that *don't* feel good (know you won't always get what you want, but you will *always* get what you need), so you can further distinguish between those things you *do* want in your lives and those things you *don't* want. Further to that, you must sometimes receive those things you don't want, that don't feel good, so you can better appreciate the situation those *around* you might have found themselves in, that you can better understand *their* situation so you might better be able to help them out of it and into a better space. That is called empathy. Do not however go down with them, not now, not ever, and no matter what. And that doesn't mean you have to drag them kicking and screaming out of the hole they might have found themselves in. It might just mean you sit on the edge and keep them company for a while, helping them not feel as bad as they might have otherwise felt. Like I said though, do not go down with them. Again, and as if you need reminding, not now, not ever, and no matter what.

Taming the Black Dog...

Darrin: Speaking of not going down with them, I knew someone who suffered from a deep depression. She took medication for it in the hope it might balance the chemicals in her body, but it didn't work (or it didn't seem to). That made me think it was an emotional problem, not a physical one, but she refused to see a counsellor or psychologist out of what seemed to be fear of facing a truth she might not have otherwise been made to face. It has been proved time and again that by facing a truth, even an unhappy one, by taking responsibility for it, you can clear some bad air around it. Why do people let things get so bad that they *can't* face it, even with the help of a professional?

The Universe: That question can apply to pretty much anything - depression, alcoholism, illness, or a physical ailment. The truth is nothing begins as something so big that it can't be dealt with easily.

It is ignored and becomes something so big it becomes *too* big to be dealt with under normal circumstances. That it does is usually a result of arrogance as much as it is ignorance on the part of the person suffering the illness or ailment, with the person thinking that the illness or ailment can never become something so big that it can't be controlled or contained. It is also a result of fear, with the person fearing that the illness or ailment may already be worse than it is and even more so that it may result in death. Please know that ignorance is *not* bliss, and to ignore the warning signs is to not trust in the message I am trying to get to them in the form of what is known as a symptom, that there is something wrong on a deeper level and it needs to be seen to immediately. The illness or ailment can also be missed by the professional or, worse still, well-hidden by the patient, which can lead to all sorts of legal issues that are above and beyond any illness or ailment being suffered by the patient. We will not discuss those legal issues here, for they are irrelevant except to say that if you do the right thing by the law, or at least don't knowingly break it, you will be fine. If you *don't* do the right thing by it, you suffer the consequences and that's how it should be. Getting back to the original question of why people let things get so bad that they can't face it, even with the help of a professional, the answer to that is to not let it in the first place, and if you can't not let it, there is an underlying problem much greater than the illness or ailment you are suffering in the now that needs to be dealt with before you can even *hope* to fix the illness or the ailment you are suffering. Get help when you need it, and don't ever be so proud, or stubborn, to think you don't.

Making Sacrifices...

Darrin: "No one who achieved anything ever sacrificed nothing." True or false?

The Universe: You don't have to sacrifice everything to achieve something, but there will come a time when you must sacrifice *something* to achieve what you want. Professional sports people sacrificed time with their friends and family to train; business people continue to sacrifice time with their families to work harder to create more business opportunities which in turn creates more money which allows them to employ others to do the work for them which in turn creates more time to do things with their families they wouldn't otherwise have; creative people, myself included, have sacrificed and continue to sacrifice relationships and friendships and nights out with friends in the continued pursuit of creative happiness. However, you need to balance what you sacrifice with what you pursue with what you do with your money and free time once you have achieved the success you so desired. Of course, you will have come across, and continue to come across, like-minded people who will make the job of balancing those things so much easier.

Why Do People Lie?

Darrin: A former friend of mine lied about something, saying she had done nothing when she had indeed done something. Why do people do this?

The Universe: They don't. They simply don't tell the truth as it is determined by the person they are talking to. That is not a lie. It is simply their version of the truth as opposed to the other person's version of the truth. That the other person's version of the truth differs does not make either version a lie. It simply makes both versions different. However, if the version of the person determined by others to have lied is based on what he has been told as opposed to what others have been told he must decide between two things: what he has been told is something he has determined to be true and fully support the person who told him regardless of what others might say, do, or think; and what he has been told is something he has determined to *not* be true and walk away from the person who told him and not look back for that person can obviously not be trusted to tell what he has determined to be the truth. However again, he must also be careful that his own version of what he has been told has not been tainted in any way or reworded to suit his own beliefs or feelings because others will determine *that* to be a lie and walk away from him and not look back for he can obviously not be trusted to tell what others have determined to be the truth.

Does My Name Define Me?

Darrin: Would I be a different person if I had a different name?

The Universe: You can only have had a different name if you were born into a different family and if you were born into a different family you would have been born into different circumstances, into a different environment, and yes to be born into a different environment would have caused you to be a different person than you are now. In fact, it would have caused you to be the person that *was* born into the environment you might otherwise have been born into. Don't think for a moment though that different means better, or that to be born into a different environment means you would have had a better life than the one you've had (or a worse one). Instead, be happy with who you are and what you've got. Just don't be satisfied with either because to be satisfied is to have come to the end of the road.

Family: Friend or Foe?

Darrin: I have chosen to spend less time with most members of my family, and none with some of them. Should I feel obligated to attend family get-togethers i.e. birthdays, Christmases etc?

The Universe: You are not obligated to do anything. If you were, you would be obligated to do everything, and no one can do everything, even though they are capable of anything. If being around family members makes you feel uncomfortable then don't be around them. Don't do it just because they think you should, and don't do it just because *you* think you should, and the only reason you will ever think you should is because *they* think you should. Do it only because it makes *you* feel good, not them, or if you know in your heart that you will feel better because of it. Otherwise, what is the point? You will feel bad for having done it, or at least less good than you did before you did it, and they will still be the same people they were that you didn't want to be around in the first place. Seems to me that while there are no winners, and nor should there be because life is not a game to be won but something to be lived, there will only be one loser, you, because you don't feel as good as you did before you went to see them and the whole point of living is to feel good because the more good you feel the more good you attract.

What is True Love?

Darrin: There are so many definitions of true love. What's yours?

The Universe: True love is the desire to be more than what you are for the good of the other person. If the other person does not share that desire, then you must give that true love to someone who does.

Don't worry that you might have wasted your time with the other person, by the way, for he or she may fully and truly appreciate what you gave them and have done for them which makes what you gave them and have done for them worth your while, but if they can't give it back, or more importantly won't, then they are not showing you the true love you are showing them (besides, to worry is to attract more things to worry about, remember?). Just walk away and find someone else, someone who will love you as truly as you will love them, and as truly as you love yourself. Stay true to that love and everything will be as it should.

Darrin: Does love really hurt as people believe it does?

The Universe: Why would it? Love is love, and to truly love someone is to experience the closest thing you will ever find to Heaven on Earth. No, what hurts is when you *lose* that love, either through death or the breakdown of a relationship. There is a line out of a Steve Martin movie called L.A. Story. It goes, "Why is it we don't know when love begins, but we always know when it ends?" Because to love in the first place means you have shed the layers of negativity which can only then mean that everything is good and one good thing therefore blends into everything else, whereas the loss of love is like pulling the foundations out from underneath a house and having the whole thing collapse to the ground. You can't always distinguish between one good thing and another, but you always know when a house has collapsed to the ground.

Darrin: And sometimes it collapses with you in it.

The Universe: Sometimes it does, and sometimes it doesn't. Sometimes it collapses on top of the one you love more than anything or anyone else in the world, and sometimes it falls causing no harm at all to anyone. You only think it does, especially when the one you think has been hurt is you.

Be the Rose, Not the Thorn…

The Universe: To most people, the rose, particularly the red rose, represents love. It is given from one person to another, usually a man to a woman, as a gesture of that love. The receiver embraces the rose, feeling the love that comes with it. But the rose, as does every good thing, has its equal and opposite, the thorn, which is sharp and capable of drawing blood if and when it comes into contact with a person's skin. People are, as they are to most things, comparable to the rose and the thorn, some capable of love and beauty, some capable of drawing blood, both literally and virtually, and some, of course, are capable of both. Be one of those that are capable of love and beauty. But don't just be *capable* of love and beauty, *be* love and beauty. *Be* the smile on another person's face. *Be* the good feeling that makes another's day. *Be* . . . the rose.

Which is Superior, Mind or Matter?

Darrin: Mark Twain once said, "Age is an issue of mind over matter. If you don't mind, it doesn't matter." This brings me to mind and matter which makes me wonder which of the two is superior. So I ask you, which one is?

The Universe: Without the mind to create it, you have no matter. Without the matter to inspire it, you have no mind. So the answer is neither. Both just are.

Darrin: What about man? Is he superior to either or both of mind and matter, or to other life forms on planet Earth, or to life on any other planet?

The Universe: Again, everything just is. As I alluded to earlier, man is no more or less superior than anything else on planet Earth or any other planet and for him to think he *is* more important is a reflection of his own inflated ego and for him to think he is *less* important is a reflection of his inability to be everything he can.

What Is The Ego?

Darrin: You speak of the ego. I myself have at times been accused, and been guilty, of having a big ego. Funny, because I never believed I did. Until I began to love truly from the heart, that is. Then I knew for sure and I set out to right a horrible wrong, to put my ego to bed once and for all. Please share with us your thoughts. What exactly is the ego and how can it affect our day to day lives?

The Universe: It is that part of you that acts as the protector of the heart, fighting back against those and that which it believes is not giving the heart everything it thinks it should. Never mind, of course, that the heart is quite capable of achieving, and therefore receiving, everything I have to offer without the help of the ego or anything else. It is also the destructive side of man that believes he is entitled to those things I have to offer others. Shame on it and shame on those who let it rule their life.

Do Those Who Have Nothing...

Darrin: Do those who have nothing ever want more than what they have, or do they accept their lot because they don't know any better?

The Universe: They may have nothing compared to you or those around you, but do they really have nothing if they have life? That doesn't mean they aren't entitled to more than what they have, of course they are and so is everyone else, it simply means that to have life, to be able to draw breath, is to have the greatest gift of all and to have the greatest gift of all is to have everything you need. What you do with that gift is then up to you.

Darrin: But those who have nothing can't do anything with that gift except exist as they are. What, then, is the point of having it if you have nothing to show for it? What, then, is the point of having it if you will *never* have anything to show for it?

The Universe: They can do almost anything they want with it. The only thing they *can't* do is what those who have plenty *can* do. But then again, maybe they're not *meant* to.

Darrin: But isn't it true that anyone can be anything they want at any time?

The Universe: Maybe they already are. Maybe they saw having nothing as a better choice for themselves than having everything and having to go through everything those with everything often have to go through to get it. And maybe they know that poor people at peace with the world are a more valuable commodity than rich people who are at war with it . . .

Sunsets and Sunrises…

Darrin: The sun rising in the east and setting in the west is more than a big ball of fire going up and down in the sky. They are picture perfect moments filled with a kaleidoscope of colours painted by the "hand of God himself". Why is it that some people can see the beauty in them and others can't? Why is it that some can see the beauty in them and others simply don't want to?

The Universe: Not everyone can and not everyone wants to. They are so caught up in their own self-pity (and as like attracts like they attract others who are caught up in their own self-pity which creates a double-whammy) they can't see the beauty in anything, let alone those things right in front of them. Fortunate are those who can. More fortunate are those who do.

Why Do We Do The Things We Do...

Darrin: Why do we do the things we do when we know that to do something else in that moment would bring us more joy, more pleasure, and probably less pain?

The Universe: First of all, does it really matter that you didn't do that something else, especially when what you could have been doing instead can still be done in the future, that you need only decide to do it and then to just do it? And more joy, more pleasure, and probably less pain that what? Than you experienced when you did what you did in that moment instead of what you could have been doing? What's to say you weren't doing what you were because it was bringing you more joy, more pleasure, and probably less pain than something *else* you could have been doing in that moment?

Don't always wonder if there is anything better you might be doing. Just know you could have been doing something worse, or what you were doing could have been worse than you believed it to be. All of a sudden you don't feel so bad, *do* you? You might even begin to feel good that what you were doing wasn't so bad after all. And it's only when you feel good that you can receive more of the same.

Bringing In the Big Bucks...

Darrin: There are so many sports stars earning so many millions of dollars a year, indeed movie stars and singers and television stars, and some sports stars, earning *tens* of millions of dollars a year, that it hardly seems fair that nurses, doctors, police officers and the like, are earning tens of *thousands* of dollars a year. Is it?

The Universe: Why wouldn't it be? It's all relevant, after all. That doctors and nurses 'only' earn tens of thousands of dollars a year for saving lives does not mean that a movie studio should not pay an actor or actress ten or twenty million dollars for a role in a movie that will probably make them two or three hundred million dollars or more, in big part because of the appearance of the actor they paid ten or twenty million dollars to play the lead role. That doctors and nurses are paid tens of thousands of dollars a year means they should probably be paid a lot more than they are, as should policemen and firemen and teachers, but they aren't, and for those who believe they should be then the better thing to do is to take your argument for more money to those who have the power to pay them more, not to argue that those who earn millions, indeed *tens* of millions, should earn less as a way of making the doctors and nurses and police officers *seem* to earn more than they do. It makes you look petty and argumentative, both of which are negatives that stop you from feeling good in any given moment and to not feel good is to stop you from receiving that which *is* good. And by the way, while the movie stars and singers and sports stars are now earning less because of the argument you've made, the teachers and doctors and police officers are still making what they were before you started it. And because they are, the question has to be asked, "What have you achieved in your argument?" The answer is, "Not much." And for those who say that at least the rich are no longer as rich as they once were, shame on your pettiness and shame on your inability to be as happy for others as you wish they would be for you.

Can Money Buy Happiness?

Darrin: Now that we know its okay for people to earn so-called "megabucks", and it is, it begs the question, "Can money buy happiness?"

The Universe: No, it can't. Indeed, it never has and never will. What it does, though, is afford you the opportunity to do more often those things that already make you happy. Let's say for example you like to travel. If you earn X amount of dollars a year and you can afford to travel once a year then you travel once a year. If, however, you earn X times ten, you can afford to travel *ten* times a year so you travel ten times a year. You like going to the movies? Go ten times as often. Of course, the other choice you have instead of going ten times as often is to take ten people on one holiday or on one visit to the movies instead. Remember though the choice is yours. Do whatever makes *you* happy.
Getting back to your question, what you need to be to be happy *after* you get the money is happy *before* you get the money. After all, if you aren't

happy *before* you get it, how can you possibly be happy *after* you get it? And if you aren't happy *after* you get it you will never be able to focus on how to create more of it and to have more of it is to be able to do more often those things that already make you happy.

A Jack of All Trades...

Darrin: There are those who are a jack of all trades but a master of none, and those who are a master of the only thing they do and have ever done and might ever do again. What is it better to be?

The Universe: Who says a jack of all trades isn't a master of any of them? And who says a master of one isn't a master of *more* than one? You? The people around you? To say any of the above is to limit one's potential, their growth, their ability to be more than they are. But then again, does it really? Or is it that they simply aren't meant to be more than they are? Maybe they have reached their full potential in their chosen field, or that they have achieved all they were meant to achieve, or all they *wanted* to achieve. And if they have, maybe it's time to move on to something else, something for which they have a greater passion than the passion they once had for what they no longer do. Move on to that and the success you achieve will be greater than the success you achieved, not because you are better at what you are doing now than anyone else but because you are better at what you are doing now than what you were doing then and you are better at what you are doing now than what you were doing then because you have a greater passion for what you are doing now than the passion you had for what you once did. Give everything you have to what you are doing now and you show me you truly want more than you have, and had, and to want more than you have is to get it. All I ask in return for you getting it is you give it back as best you know how. And I don't mean to me personally. I mean that you take the $40000 I gave you and buy a brand new car for $30000 and give $10000 to a charity instead of buying a brand new car for $40000 and giving nothing to anyone else. That I ever gave you $40000 means I trust you to do just that. That I ever gave anything to *anyone* means I trust them to do just that with what I gave them.

Darrin: My gratitude for the trust you have in me is greater than it will ever be for the $40000 you gave me, and please know I will be forever grateful for the $40000 which is not only more than I had but having more than I had is exactly what I wanted. So thank you.

The Universe: You are welcome.

The Things We Have Done...

Darrin: If I may, I would like to change the subject now from what we can be instead of what we were to what we have done. More specifically, what *I* have done. In a moment of weakness, I cheated on a past partner. Why do we do such things, and while I know my life could have been made worse for having had the experience, can it possibly have been made better for having had the experience (and I don't mean to cheat is to create a better life, but to have the experience then learn from it which in itself might help to create it)?

The Universe: First of all, you have excused your behaviour as a moment of weakness instead of accepting it for what it really is, cheating on the person you loved, the person you had given yourself to for better or worse. Second of all, why are you even thinking about it? Worse still, *worrying* about it? To do either means you are still holding onto that moment, to that experience, to that feeling. Do yourself and those around you now a favour and let it go. Beating yourself up over something that has already happened won't make it go away. It will only stop you from receiving everything good that I have to offer you in the now. That's the lesson to learn and to learn it is to create the better life you so desire.

Why Are We Afraid To Make Mistakes?

Darrin: If we learn from our mistakes, and we do eventually if not straight away, why are we so afraid to make them?

The Universe: Because you worry what others will say when you do, that they will judge you or make fun of you. I've no doubt they will but that is a reflection of them not you, so why worry if they *do* judge you or make fun of you? You also worry that you will be worse off emotionally, financially or physically. You might be worse off in that moment but to concern yourself with such things as those things I've just mentioned is to forget everything I have taught you thus far that boils down to one thing, that to not feel good in any one moment is to stop yourself receiving more good.

Feel good even when you make a mistake, admit you made one, and make amends. Once you have done that, get on with your day, your week, your month, your life. And do it with a smile on your face. The other side of the coin is that people are not as worried about making a mistake as they are that they might actually succeed, that they might be *better off* emotionally, financially or physically and to succeed is to be more than what they were taught they *could* be by those who came before them, and to be more than that is to step outside their comfort zone, one in which they were pushed from pillar to post, held back and held down, and had their minds poisoned. Looks to me their comfort zone isn't so comfortable after all and they should get out of it as fast as possible. Grab the bull by the horns and run like the wind, my friends.

Why Am I Me and Not Someone Else?

Darrin: Elvis Presley once wondered why he and not someone else had been born into the body of the man who many would one day proclaim to be the King of rock and roll. I've sometimes wondered why I and not someone else had been born into *my* body. The question is, "Why am I me and not someone else, and why is someone else not me?"

The Universe: You are all who you are, and in all reality you would only want to be someone else if you perceived their life to be better than yours or yours to be worse than theirs (and is your life really that bad that you would want to take that chance?). And if you were someone else and asked the same question, you would still be the one asking it. Therefore, you cannot ever be 'someone else', nor they you. You can only ever be you and they can only ever be them. And instead of wondering why you aren't someone else, be happy with who you are. Just don't be satisfied with who you are because, as I said in my answer to your earlier question about names defining people, to be satisfied is to have come to the end of the road.

Are Things Really That Easy?

Darrin: Some people, Elvis Presley for example, are so good at something they make it look easy. Is it?

The Universe: It's certainly not hard. Nothing is. It's only made to *seem* hard by your belief in other people's disbelief in themselves and of you. As long as you maintain your belief in the only thing that's true – that you can have, do and be anything you want, whenever you want (as long as you are willing to work for it or at the very least give something in return for it) – and as long as you give everything to those things that make you feel good, you too can make what you do look easy.

Answering Questions with a Question...

Darrin: We are told not to answer a question with a question, yet an answer in the form of another question will make them think of an answer to *your* question, whereas an answer in the form of an answer will not, as there's no need because they already *have* the answer and they have it because you gave it to them (unless, of course, they want a different one to the one you've given them in which case they will ask for a different answer or come up with one of their own). What's better then, to answer a question with an answer or to answer it with another question?

The Universe: If you are a psychologist or philosopher or counsellor or such, the better way to do it is to answer their question with a question of your own. That way you make them think for themselves instead of them relying on others for the answer to their question and that is what psychologists and philosophers and counsellors and such are here for, to help people think for themselves instead of those same people relying on others for the answers. However, if for example you are a child responding to a parent, it is probably best to give them a straight answer, especially if the answer is a response to something like a request for the truth. That said, it doesn't hurt for a child to be made to think for themselves either, for the sooner someone is made to do that the sooner they can think for themselves and the sooner they can think for themselves the less likely they are to grow up having had others think *for* them and when others do the thinking they are usually thinking not for and of others, but for and of themselves.

Has The End Ever Justified The Means?

Darrin: Some people will do whatever it takes. They will perform illegal and immoral acts to get what they want. They excuse their behaviour by saying the end justifies the means. Does it really?

The Universe: Anything that has ever happened has been a direct result of something that happened before it. It is also a prelude to and the cause of the very next thing that happens after it. As a result, there has never been, nor will there ever be, an end to anything and their excuse is exactly that, an excuse, and a poor one at that for it does nothing but paper over a crack in the wall that unless tended to might see the wall come down on top of them.

What Are Dreams?

Darrin: What are dreams, and what part do they play in the bigger picture?

The Universe: Dreams are the subconscious's way of going through the day's thoughts and filtering them into several groups. Some of those thoughts it files away for future reference, some it brings up to the conscious level for immediate or very near future use, and others it is dumping and burning, never to be seen or heard of again. Some dreams are as real as if they were taking place in every day life. Others are remembered but soon forgotten. Others still are never remembered. Many, be they remembered or not, will play out in real life in one way or another. They will help guide you to where you are meant to be. And some of them, you call them 'nightmares', will take you away from where you're *not* meant to be by showing you why you're not meant to be there.

Darrin: Are we, as a people, the dream come true of someone, or something, that came before us?

The Universe: You are *my* dream come true, and you are everything I hoped you would be.

Darrin: Even those who aren't being everything they *can* be?

The Universe: You are all being everything I need you to be in any given moment, and that's all that matters.

A Matter of Opinion...

Darrin: Some people are better known for producing poor pieces of work than those who have created masterpieces. Why?

The Universe: Who says a piece of work is poor or otherwise? Is that not just an opinion? And what makes a piece of work poor or otherwise in their opinion? What people are willing to pay for it or not? That would make most pieces of art created by

Jackson Pollock, pieces of art that have sold for tens of millions of dollars, masterpieces yet many critics have scoffed at them. Indeed, art critic Howard Devree once referred to Pollock's work as "baked macaroni". Don't ever base your own opinion of something on the opinion of someone else. Be guided by it, yes. But don't ever base your own on it. Think of how much good you might miss out on if you did.

What to Do Before I Die...

Darrin: Some people I know have constructed a "bucket list", a list of things to do before they die. Is this a good idea?

The Universe: Is it a bad one? The answer to both is no. It's not a good idea because you may not get to do all of the things on your list and on your deathbed might therefore look back on your life in regret which is not a good thing. And it *is* a good idea because it gives you something to focus on, to strive for. But even that's not so good because if you focus too much on going on an African safari or jumping out of a plane you might miss the job opportunity or chance to meet the person that affords you the chance to do those things you are focusing on. Better to create a list of things you want and want to do, then set out to do the things you *need* to do. Everything else will fall into place, just as it should.

Something to Complain About...

Darrin: No matter how nice the day, no matter how nice the people around them are, people will always find something to complain about in their life, or the lives of those around them, like how sick they are, or even how well they are (and how crazy is it to complain about how well you are?). Why do they do it?

The Universe: Because they will always complain, even when there's nothing to complain about (if there's nothing to complain about they will create it). That's what they do, because having something to complain about simply allows them to justify their continued need to complain and their continued need to complain has been brought about by their belief in other people's disbelief in themselves and of those around them, and the shame that their belief in other people's disbelief in themselves and of those around them has been allowed to become greater than their heart's desire.

Blood, Guts and Gore...

Darrin: If someone hurts me, is it nobler to kill them or to suffer their abuse?

The Universe: Neither. That said, you are well entitled to protect and defend yourself. Just know your reaction must never be greater than the other person's action. Once it is, their reaction might very well be greater than yours as yours was to their initial action. And once it is, the question goes from being how much can we take to how much can we give. Better just to walk away.

Darrin: Why are people who will never kill or rape or burn things to the ground attracted to stories, real or otherwise, of people who have killed or raped or burned things to the ground?

The Universe: Just because they will never kill or rape or burn things to the ground doesn't mean they aren't capable of it, and just because they are attracted to stories, real or otherwise, of people who have killed or raped or burned things to the ground doesn't mean they are going to do it. They want to be entertained, and as some people are more entertained by a game of football than they are by a game of chess, and visa versa, some people are more entertained by stories, real or otherwise, of people who have killed or raped or burned things to the ground than they are of stories, real or otherwise, of love or drama or of those set in the old west. The human race will always want to be more than what it is, and if what it is in any given moment is better entertained than it was in any *previous* moment that can only be a good thing as far as they are concerned and if what it is in any given moment is better entertained than it was in any *previous* moment that can only be a good thing as far as *I* am concerned.

Darrin: There are innumerable tales of men and women, of fathers and mothers, killing those closest to them. They shoot their wives or husbands, throw their children off bridges, then, to make it even worse, kill themselves and they do it I believe to avoid justice being served on them. Why do they kill those closest to them, then more often than not kill themselves soon after?

The Universe: There is such a thing as the Law of Opposites that says for every action there is an equal and opposite reaction. That Law can be applied to people as equally as it can to anything else, that for every good man there is also a bad one. Sometimes they are one and the same. Those men and women were not *born* bad, even those who have committed the most heinous crimes. Nothing is ever born "bad". They are simply born into bad environments. Or, in the case of good men and women who turn bad, find themselves in bad environments they can't get out of and they see death as their only way out (that does not of course excuse them killing their children or their husband or wife). By the way, there is no such thing as good people doing bad things. If you do something bad, you are in that moment a bad person. But that doesn't mean you are always bad, just in that moment.

Darrin: What about suicide? What about those that kill themselves with or without having killed another?

The Universe: Western religions, particularly the Catholic Church, say you will go to Hell if you commit suicide, that you have removed God's will and made it your own. But how can you go there if it doesn't exist? That doesn't make suicide right, or even wrong. It means that religious people have fooled others and have been fooled themselves into thinking they can and can't do certain things because God said so. Indeed, those in the Middle East, those who are most likely to take religion to its extreme (that is not an opinion but fact), are led to believe that to kill others in the process of killing themselves will give them eternal life in a very happy place surrounded by very happy people. The only truth in killing others in the process of killing yourself is that you end their life as early as you ended yours and you leave their family and friends without a husband or wife or son or daughter or work colleague or golf partner. I will not punish you for doing that for that's not what I do. You will however come back to planet Earth to live life over and over again until you have learned the lessons you set out to learn, one of them being that to kill someone is wrong unless it's in self-defence, even then it should only be a last resort. The bottom line is that committing suicide is not and never has been against any law and you will not go to Hell for doing it. What will happen though if you do commit suicide? You will miss out on the rest of what could have been a very happy existence, and those around you i.e. friends and family, will be losing a part of themselves because to lose someone close to you, whichever way you do, is to lose a part of you. And don't think for a moment you will be avoiding what you believe will have been a horrible and sad life, because you will surely be born back into it, time after time after time until you have learned the lessons you set out to learn.

Now you know there is no escaping life, you may as well live it. And if you are going to live it you may as well make the most of it because the more you make of it the better the next one will be and the better it is the less likely it is that you need to keep coming back.

If a Tree Falls in the Forest...

Darrin: If a tree falls in the forest and no one's around to hear it, *does* it make a sound?

The Universe: Does it matter? No. All that matters is the question came about so it might take your mind off what you are thinking about. So, if you are thinking about how poor you are or how bad your day has been or how bad your life is and your attention is turned to whether or not a falling tree makes a sound if no one is around to hear it, you will no longer be thinking about how poor you are or how bad your day has been or how bad your life is and that can only be a good thing, and good things beget good thoughts of *more* good things which begets more good things. Of course, don't go crazy not knowing the answer to the question, because there isn't one, just as there is no answer to any question whose job it is to take your mind off how poor you are or how bad your day has been or how bad your life is and as long as it does that its job is done.

Controlling Population Growth…

Darrin: Are cancer, AIDS and other illnesses and diseases your way of controlling population growth on planet Earth?

The Universe: I have never once set out to control anything, let alone introducing something that would cause anyone grief of any kind, especially not *this* much grief. That said, the population growth on your planet *is* unsustainable and while the men and women who have created and introduced diseases such as AIDS were placed there by me and while the idea that the population growth on your planet is unsustainable has been placed in people's minds by me the idea to create and introduce diseases such as AIDS is solely that of the men and women who created and introduced it.

Darrin: But if everything begins and ends with you, and I believe it does, aren't you responsible for everything that happens in between?

The Universe: And your life begins and ends with you, but you are not responsible for anything that happens in between, only your *reaction* to the things that happen, so while the men and women who created and introduced diseases such as AIDS were placed on planet Earth by me, so were the men and women who will create and introduce the *cures* to cancer and AIDS. That is my reaction to the actions of the men and women who created and introduced diseases such as AIDS and illnesses such as cancer to the human race.

Mankind's Greatest Achievement...

Darrin: What is it?

The Universe: In spite of what has been achieved thus far, and what has been achieved thus far is mind-blowing to say the least, it is yet to come, and believe me, you will know when it does.

Male, Female, and Homosexuality...

Darrin: Does a person's gender affect the outcome of their daily life, or is gender nothing more than the difference between two people who come together to create the next generation of the human race?

The Universe: Yes to both. How much though someone lets it affect the outcome of their daily life and in what way depends on the person being affected. They can either let it or not. If they let it they can let it a lot or a little. Be warned though that anything attracts more of itself and more of anything attracts even more. Therefore, better to not let it at all, or if you do to only let it affect your daily life in positive ways. Also, in spite of what some members of the human race will tell you, and those members are more often than not the ones who will try and affect the outcome of another's daily life, gender really is nothing more than the difference between two people who come together to create the next generation of the human race.

Darrin: Is homosexuality and lesbianism right or wrong?

The Universe: In the eyes of the Catholic Church it is wrong. In the eyes of those who are labelled homosexuals and lesbians it is right, or at the very least it is what it is and they just go about their daily lives. To those who are neither it probably doesn't matter. About the only thing I can find "wrong" with it is that one person of a particular sex can't get another person of the same sex pregnant. Then again, what's to say my reaction to the world becoming homosexual instead of being heterosexual won't be to introduce a man or woman to planet Earth who will know how to get someone of one particular sex pregnant by someone else of the same sex, just as I introduced the men and women to planet Earth who will create and introduce the cures to cancer and AIDS?

Cannibalism...

Darrin: Several years ago I watched a movie about a rugby team whose plane crashed in the Andes. The survivors of the crash were left several days later with no choice but to eat the flesh of those who had died or they would likely die themselves. Is it wrong for one human being to eat the flesh of another?

The Universe: Not if someone is lost in the mountains and will surely starve to death unless they eat the flesh of their already dead mate. What *is* wrong is for them to kill their mate for their mate's flesh so they themselves might survive at their mate's expense. That is murder, and murder is against the law as the human race has written it. Indeed, that there are still people in the world who will kill another person for no particular reason and eat their flesh shows the human race as a whole still has a long way to go.

Religion and Philosophy...

Darrin: What part, if any, does religion play in philosophy, and what part does philosophy play in religion?

The Universe: Neither plays any part in the other, for both are nothing more than words. What *does* play a part in both is a person's belief in what he has been taught in the past and what he will be taught in the future. Even more so, in what is happening right now. And if you have been raised in a family where both parents went to church every week chances are you went too, might still do, and chances are you will simply accept the church's word about what is real and what is not, what happened and what is yet to come, and so on. Or if you were raised in a family where both parents searched every moment of every day for what they knew in their heart was a better life and the answers that would help them find it, you are probably inclined to follow their footsteps and those who walk that path are called philosophers, whether they know it or not, whether they think of themselves as such or not. Believe in one or the other or both or neither, but please don't put either, or both, down because to do so is a negative action and anything negative stops you from receiving all the good you are entitled to. Remember?

Karma...

Darrin: What about karma? What is it, and is it real?

The Universe: Karma is the word used to describe the coming back at you from another that which you gave to them. "What goes around comes around." "What you give, you get back." When you think about it that way, it is really a word that describes the Law of Opposites, that for every action there is an equal and opposite reaction. I don't mean by giving out good you get back bad or visa versa (though it can and does happen), but what you give out you do get back. You have sent it out and the equal and opposite reaction is that it comes back to you, every time. And seeing as the

Law of Opposites is as real as any other law and at work every moment of every day of every week of every month of every year, you best give out the best you possibly can.

Visualization...

Darrin: Proponents of the Law of Attraction say that for it to truly work, you must, among other things, visualize having what you want. Does visualization really work?

The Universe: Not in the sense that if you visualize something it will magically turn up on your doorstep like some people seem to think it does. You have to believe in it and want it like you've never wanted anything else in your life. And you have to work for it, sometimes very hard. Only then will visualization work (remember though that the Law of Attraction is always working whether you believe it or not and regardless of what you visualize). Even then, what turns up might not be exactly what you hoped would or exactly what you visualized. That doesn't mean your visualizations didn't work. After all, you wanted a car, you got a car. That you got a Mercedes Benz instead of a BMW or a holiday to

Europe instead of America (or visa versa) is irrelevant. Isn't it?

Darrin: "Be happy with what you get." Then why aren't they?

The Universe: Because they didn't get all they wanted. But again, if you were meant to get more than you did, you would have. And just because you didn't get it now doesn't mean you weren't meant to get it at all. It means you might have got it later. Of course, there *is* the chance you weren't meant to get it at all, that someone else needed it more than you, or that someone else would have put it to better use or looked after it better. And of course, whilst ever you aren't happy with what you get, you'll *never* get everything you want.

Meditation...

Darrin: What is meditation and how does it work?

The Universe: It is the relaxing of one's mind and body and the consequent connecting to an inner peace that you have no other way of connecting to which will then allow you to communicate more peacefully with whatever it is you believe is higher than yourself, be it God or The Universe or your guardian angels. Of course, there is nothing to stop you from communicating with those things while you are *not* meditating. It is simply easier to do so while you are for all outside interferences are disregarded at that time.

Knowledge...

Darrin: What is the point, if there is one, of knowing everything, or, indeed, anything at all?

The Universe: While you are armed with everything you will ever need, you, as a human being, will never know everything. Not all at once anyway. If you did, it would do nothing but confuse you. Besides, there is no need to know everything at all let alone all at once, only those things you need to get through each moment and those things you need to get from wherever you are in any given moment to wherever it is you want or need to be. To answer the second part of your question, to know nothing at all is to step in front of a moving car because you don't know it's coming, or you don't know the damage it will do to your body when it hits it. Instead, you step out of the way and you do so because you heard the car coming and because you know it's the sensible thing to do, and even though those who raised you might have poisoned your mind with things that haven't served you, they never poisoned it that much that you didn't know to step out of the way of a moving car.

Inner Beauty...

Darrin: I have seen and heard them all and have come to the conclusion that beautiful people are nothing without a beautiful heart.

The Universe: There are so many people in this world whose good looks melt hearts all over the place, and then they open their mouth, proving to the world that as beautiful as they are on the outside they are nothing to look at on the inside, that their hearts are nothing compared to their looks, that their ability to hurt with a single lash of the tongue is comparable to a knockout punch from a heavyweight boxer. Beware for your own sake the beautiful person without a beautiful heart, and embrace the person with a beautiful heart regardless of their looks for the person with a beautiful heart is more beautiful than the beautiful person without a beautiful heart will ever be, and the more beautiful the person the more beautiful your relationship with them, and the more beautiful your relationship with them the more beautiful your relationship with yourself, and the more beautiful your relationship with yourself the more beautiful your relationship with them, and so it goes.

I Am My Own Person...

Darrin: Unless they paid for me, which they didn't, they don't own me. Not now, not ever.

The Universe: As much as people like to *think* they do, they don't own you. They like to think they can control you, telling you what to do, where to go, what to say, and what to wear, but they can't, *unless you let them.* So the answer is simple – don't let them. You are the creator of your own destiny and are responsible for who you are and who you become, and you, no one else, are the one with the voice that has the power to change your world. Use it to your best advantage and do change your world, but remember this – as they don't own you, you don't own them. Remember that, and you let go of the need to control others which frees you to control yourself which allows you to become what you truly are – the creator, and therefore master, of your own destiny, and the creator, and therefore master, of your own reality.

How Far Can You Push Your Luck?

Darrin: The only way to know how far you can push your luck is to push it as far as you can. Correct?

The Universe: There is no other way. You must continue to push yourselves beyond what you thought (read, what you were taught by others) was possible, always striving for more, always creating more of what you already are and have. To do that you must take chances. You must leave your comfort zone. You must take a leap of faith into the unknown and find that place as a racing car driver does where you will get most traction in your life without going off the track and when you find it and have gained the traction you so desire you must push hard and then even harder, always striving for that fraction of a second extra speed that over a period of time will add up to seconds and minutes and hours advantage over your rivals, the greatest of which is who you once were. Always be better than who you once were and also who you are now, and you do that by pushing your luck, and you push your luck as far as you can or you don't bother pushing it at all.

Mending a Broken Heart...

The Universe: It's all about forgiveness. Learning how to forgive someone when they break your heart, and then actually doing it, is to let go of the need to dislike them or hate them or get revenge on them, all of which are energy-draining thoughts and emotions that will ultimately hurt no one but you. As for doing or saying or thinking anything that's not positive, the more energy you give those things the less energy you have to give the things that will actually serve a purpose in your life and the less energy you give to those things that will actually serve a purpose in your life the more energy you end up giving to disliking or hating or getting revenge on the person who broke your heart. It's like being in a car with no brakes that you've aimed at a brick wall at a hundred miles an hour. Sooner or later you will hit that wall and it's going to hurt like hell. Better to get out of the car before it hits. Better still to not get in the car in the first place. Give your energy instead to those things that will serve a purpose in your life and your life will go ahead in leaps and bounds and your once broken heart will go with it, leaving behind the hurt and pain that caused it to break in the first place. And not only will your life go ahead in leaps and bounds, it will go in the direction you want it to.

Unlocking the Door...

Darrin: I am the key to unlocking and opening my own door. I know that. I also know if the key doesn't fit the door I'm trying to open, or once did but no longer does, I need to either change the key or change the door. That's not always an easy thing to do.

The Universe: No its not, but there's no point in banging your head against a brick wall. You'll only end up hurting your head. The unfortunate thing is you are programmed by your environment to accept what is no matter how obvious it is that what is might be wrong for you and it's time you accepted not what is but your inability to *change* what is and when you accept that you can't change what is you allow yourselves the opportunity to change how you *react* to what is and by changing how you *react* to what is you inadvertently change what is and it's different because you are reacting differently to it. How good is it to know that what was no longer is and all it took for that to happen was for you to react differently to it?

Be the Creator of a Bold New World...

The Universe: You are all God-like in that you have the ability to create whatever you want, whenever you want, and however you want. As a people, you have created vehicles to move yourselves from where you are to wherever you want to be, anywhere in the world; you have created communication devices that allow yourselves to talk to and see people on the other side of town, the other side of the country, and the other side of the planet, all at the same time; and as people you can create a world all of your own in which you can do, be, and have anything you want.

"Really?" I hear you ask to the last of those three examples.

Those who have already created their world know it is possible, and those who haven't even started haven't started out of fear or laziness or any other reason or excuse they can think of. And please don't say *can't* because you always *can*. You can become a doctor if you want to, or a professional sportsperson, or anything else you put your mind to. You may of course never become any of those things or anything else, but let it be because you chose to become something else instead, and when you are on your way to becoming that something else you are on your way to creating a bold new world . . . yours.

I Choose to Question What Others Think...

Darrin: I choose to question what others think of as normal if what others think of as normal feels wrong for me.

The Universe: You have no idea how happy I am to hear that because how many times have drinkers of alcohol looked at you as if you are from another planet when you tell them you don't drink even though you know not to drink is what's best for you? What about followers of rugby league or gridiron or basketball when you tell them you have no interest in sport or, worse still in their eyes, that your chosen sport is something so far removed from rugby league or gridiron or basketball that you must surely have been dropped on your head at birth? What is normal to them is not always even *right* for them and it certainly is not always right for you. Most people follow the leader (who says to drink alcohol or follow a sport where men simply run headfirst into each other is to prove you are a man) because they lack the courage to go their own way, to blaze a trail rather than follow one as Ralph Waldo Emerson once said. Dare to step off the beaten path, which in itself shows an abundance of courage that will serve you well in practically every area of your life, create a new life for yourself (the one you want instead of the one others want for you) which in turns creates a happiness within you that attracts happy people that add to your already happy feeling which attracts even *happier* people (and those happier people might be the same happy people you attracted earlier who are now simply happier than they were before) and soon you will find yourself having gone from a group of people whose definition of what is normal is too different from yours to a group of like-minded people capable of helping you further along your chosen path. It could then be said that blazing a trail does not necessarily mean going it alone (which is the main reason people choose to follow the leader because they think to blaze a trail *is* to go it alone and perish the thought that you would ever actually do that), rather that you blaze a trail from the one you were on to the one on which like-minded people are *also* on. Questioning what others think of as normal if what is normal to others feels wrong for you then getting the courage to step off their path and onto your own then actually doing it doesn't seem like such a crazy thing to do after all, does it?

Let Them Be, Or Let Them Go...

The Universe: To give yourself to one person means that person must first want to receive you, and unless they are willing to receive you as you are it is not worth being with that person for they will chop you and change you and turn you into what they will tell you is the person you *can* be, when what they are *really* doing is chopping you and changing you into the person they really want to be with. They should spare a thought for you and either let you be or let you go. If they choose to let you be they must realize now and in the future they have made the choice to accept you as you are all by themselves and they must then accept you for all your good and also all your faults and if the time comes that they can't, if it hasn't come already, they must let you go for all time and move on to someone who is already the person they want to be with. If on the other hand you allow yourself to give up on those things that make you who you are just so you can be with someone you are destined to become unhappy with who you become and if you are unhappy with who you become it is a sure bet the other person soon will be too. When that happens you have two unhappy people in a relationship that is then doomed, a relationship that may otherwise have flourished had both you and the other person maintained who you are and both accepted who the other one is . . . and isn't that what you both want, a relationship that will flourish?

Wanting To Know and Needing To Know…

The Universe: You might *want* to know, but do you really *need* to know? Curiosity is a strange thing in that it makes people want to know things that usually aren't their business and would usually do them no good to know anyway.

People spend so much time and energy wanting to know something that they lose sight of what they *need* to know and its what they *need* to know that gets them from where they are to where they are meant to be. Sure, what they *want* to know might get them closer to their destination than not knowing at all, but if you let go of what you *want* to know and focus on finding out those things you *need* to know you will reach your destination much faster than you otherwise would, and isn't that what you want?

A Fork in the Road...

The Universe: Somewhere on your chosen path you will come to a fork in the road where what you thought you would have forever will go one way while you go the other. You will think for a moment about turning away from your destination to follow what you thought you would have forever, especially if what you thought you would have forever is a person, but you must perish the thought for by going in a different direction to what you thought you would have forever is that which you thought you would have forever simply following its *own* path to its *own* destination just as you must stay on *your* path to *your* destination. Besides, who says the paths don't meet up again somewhere down the track?

Don't Let The Sun Go Down...

The Universe: Don't ever let the sun go down on who or what you want to be, but first you have to decide who and what you want to be, then set out and become that person. That said, of course, if who or what you want to be is immoral or someone who does illegal things then expect the police to stand in your way, and they will, and so they should. But if who and what you want to be is capable of amazing and wonderful and loving things then you stand tall against those who would stand in your way (and they stand in your way for no other reason than they are incapable of becoming that person themselves) and you become that person, come Hell or high water, and once you have become that person you will know, even if you can't see it yet, that it was worth going through the things you did to become the person you have.

Give Everything You Have...

Darrin: A good friend once told me to give everything I have to what I want, that way I have nothing left to give to what I *don't* want . . .

The Universe: So many people give so much to what they *don't* want they lose sight of what they *do* want then complain they have lost sight of what they want. Stop right there. Change your focus to what you *do* want – a happy relationship, a good job, a holiday – and give everything to it, and always focus on the end result. Avoid distractions, and they will come, at all costs and you do that by continuing to give everything you have to what you want. You will lose friends, probably even your job or a relationship with a loved one, but it is just as important to remember this as it is to remember to give everything you have to what you want: "Good things fall over so better things can take their place." Remember that and you remember everything you need to know in the one moment when friends, jobs and relationships are lost, when those who are destined to fail turn to giving everything they have to what they *don't* want, and those who are destined to succeed continue to give everything they have to what they *do* want.

Draw A Line In The Sand And Cross It…

Darrin: I have drawn a line between now and then and crossed it, and I am prepared to go on without them if they can't or won't cross it themselves.

The Universe: It is of vital importance to live in the now, to enjoy what you have now as opposed to wasting your time wishing you had what you didn't have then, because to live in the now allows you to create now what you wish you had now that you didn't have then, and if those around you now who were a part of your past can't do the same it is time to let them go so you may create the future you wish you had created in the past. Leave them to deal with their own demons as best they can, knowing full well you have already dealt with yours and because you have and because they won't or can't or haven't you are entitled to move on if that's what you choose to do. Be brave, move into the future, and be even *more* brave and move into the future on your own if that's what you have to do, for somewhere in the future, guaranteed, you will find the people who have already crossed *their* line in the sand, people who have also left the past behind and embraced the future with both hands, and isn't that what you wanted, someone who has crossed the line into the now?

Be Your Own Superhero...

The Universe: There is a part of each and every one of you who wants to be a hero to someone, to help them out of the space they are in and you do it for one of two reasons, you want someone to love you, or for someone to love you more than they already do. Please perish the thought that being a hero to someone will cause them to love you more than they already do or even to love you at all. Start by being a hero to yourself. Help *yourself* out of the space *you* are in, and its when you are in a better space that you will find someone who will love you and if they already love you that's when they will love you more, and if they don't love you or love you more you will attract someone who will, and they will love you for the right reasons, not because you can be a hero to them but because you were a hero to yourself, and to be a hero to one's self is to show the world that nothing and no one can bring you down, not even you, and there is nothing more attractive to a potential mate than their potential mate being everything to themselves they can possibly be, because to be everything to one's self shows the potential and the ability to be everything to others, and as the Law of Attraction says: "Like attracts like", so by giving out the ability to be everything to others you must and will attract those with the ability to be everything to you. How good is it to know you are now able to attract that kind of person into your life? How much better than that is it to know that while they can be everything to you if you need them to be, you don't *need* them to be because you are already everything to yourself?

A Final Word from The Universe to You: Consider yourselves better prepared now than you once were, so go forth and create the life you are entitled to, and thank you for being everything you are, and for playing so well the part you are perfect for, the one you were literally born to play.

Peace to you all and love to each and every one of you.

ABOUT THE AUTHOR

Darrin Mason has worked much of his adult life as a freelance cartoonist (he is an **Australian Cartoon Award** winner) whose work has appeared in a number of Australian newspapers and magazines (**People magazine** and **The Truth** newspaper to name but two) and as a producer at **4BC** radio in Brisbane, Australia. Most important of all, he is a fan of Batman (the 1960s TV version, the late 1980s/early 1990s Michael Keaton version, and the Christian Bale trilogy. You can forget the rest). As the Metallica song goes, nothing else matters.

Visit **www.darrinmason.com** for more books by this author and to sign up for our newsletter.

NOTES

NOTES

NOTES

NOTES

NOTES

NOTES

NOTES